Ants

and Other Social Insects

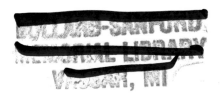

Concept and Product Development: Editorial Options, Inc.
Series Designer: Karen Donica
Book Author: Cecilia Venn

For information about other World Book publications, visit our
Web site at **http://www.worldbook.com**, or call **1-800-WORLDBK (967-5325)**.
For information about sales to schools and libraries, call **1-800-975-3250**
(United States); 1-800-837-5365 (Canada).

2004 printing

World Book, Inc.
233 North Michigan Avenue
Chicago, IL 60601

The Library of Congress has cataloged an earlier edition on this title as follows:

Library of Congress Cataloging-in-Publication Data

Venn, Cecilia.
    Ants and other social insects / [book author, Cecilia Venn].
      p. cm.—(World Book's animals of the world)
    Summary: Questions and answers explore the world of social insects, with an emphasis
on ants.
    ISBN 0-7166-1205-4 -- ISBN 0-7166-1200-3 (set)
     1. Ants—Juvenile literature. 2. Insect societies—Juvenile literature. [1. Ants—Miscellanea.
2. Insect societies—Miscellanea. 3. Insects—Miscellanea. 4. Questions and answers.] I. World
Book, Inc. II. Title. III. Series.
    QL568.F7 V43 2000
    595.79'6—dc21
                                          00-021632
This edition: ISBN: 0-7166-1238-0; ISBN: 0-7166-1237-2 (set)

Printed in Malaysia

3 4 5 6 7 8 9 05 04

Picture Acknowledgments: Cover: © David Dennis, Tom Stack & Associates; © R. J. Erwin, Photo Researchers; © David
Overcash, Bruce Coleman Inc.; © C. Brad Simmons, Bruce Coleman Inc.; © Kenneth H. Thomas, Photo Researchers.

© M. & R. Borland, Bruce Coleman Inc. 27; © Scott Camazine, Photo Researchers 17; © J. C. Carton, Bruce Coleman Inc. 57;
© Stephen Dalton, Photo Researchers 25; © Treat Davidson, Photo Researchers 37; © David Dennis, Tom Stack & Associates 3, 31;
© Gregory Dimijian, Photo Researchers 33, 35; © R. J. Erwin, Photo Researchers 4, 61; © Jeff Foott, Bruce Coleman Inc. 19, 51;
© David Overcash, Bruce Coleman Inc. 29; © John W. Mitchell, Bruce Coleman Inc. 11; © Harry Rogers/NAS from Photo
Researchers 53; © C. Brad Simmons, Bruce Coleman Inc. 47; © Kim Taylor, Bruce Coleman Inc. 5, 13, 43, 45; © Kenneth H.
Thomas, Photo Researchers 5, 21, 49; © R. Van Nostrand, Photo Researchers 39; © Peter Ward, Bruce Coleman Inc. 55; © L. West,
Bruce Coleman Inc. 4, 41, 59; © Paul A. Zahl, Photo Researchers 7.

Illustrations: WORLD BOOK illustration by Michael DiGiorgio 15, 23; WORLD BOOK illustration by Patricia Stein 9, 62.

Ants

and Other Social Insects

Mmm! Who wants a fungus sandwich?

World Book, Inc.
A Scott Fetzer Company
Chicago

Contents

Why do I wag my tail?

How can we be so strong if we are so tiny?

How do I mind my own beeswax?

Who lives in a paper house?

What Is a
Social Insect?

Ants are social insects. So are termites, many bees, and some wasps. Social insects have a real family life. They live in communities, and the members of a community depend on one another.

There are more than a million different species, or kinds, of insects in the world. Insects include beetles, crickets, butterflies, and houseflies. Insects come in many different shapes, sizes, and colors. But there are some things that all insects have in common. They all have six legs and bodies that are divided into three main parts. They all have tough, shell-like body coverings. And most, but not all, have wings.

Ants, termites, bees, and wasps may look a lot like these other insects. But as social insects, they lead very different lives.

Amazon ant

Where in the World Do Social Insects Live?

There are about 10,000 species of ants. So it is not surprising that ants, like millions of other social insects, live everywhere on land, except where it is really cold. In fact, areas with warm and moist climates have the most types of ants and other insects.

Tropical rain forests are very rich in insect life. If all the animals in the Amazon rain forest were weighed, many scientists think ants and termites would make up one-third of that weight.

Ants are successful survivors. They have different ways of life that allow them to live in different habitats. And their small size makes it easy for them to find food and shelter.

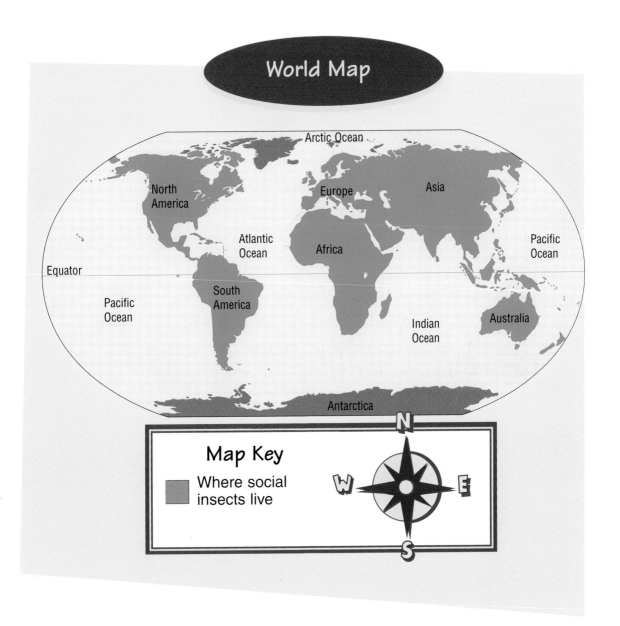

World Map

Arctic Ocean

North America

Europe

Asia

Atlantic Ocean

Africa

Pacific Ocean

Equator

Pacific Ocean

South America

Indian Ocean

Australia

Antarctica

Map Key

Where social insects live

N

W

E

S

Why Are Ants
Social Insects?

Ants are social insects because they live and work together in communities. Here, they feed and protect one another. They raise and care for their young. This way of life is very different from that of solitary insects that spend most, and sometimes all, of their lives alone.

An ant community is called a colony *(KAHL uh nee)*. Life in an ant colony is very organized. Each member has a job to do, from laying eggs to gathering food to fighting.

For most ants, colony life centers around the nest. The nest may be underground, in a mound, or even among the treetops. When ants build a nest, the dirt that piles up around the entrance forms an anthill.

An ant colony is a very busy place. It can also be very crowded. There may be hundreds, thousands, or even millions of ants in a single colony!

Anthill

Who's Who in an Ant Colony?

Like most social insects, ants have three castes, or classes. There are queen ants, worker ants, and male ants.

A queen does not rule the colony, but she is an important member. She has one job—to lay eggs. Without her, a colony would die out. The reason is that only the queens in most species of ants can reproduce. They also live the longest—10 to 20 years. A colony may have one or more queens. A European wood ant mound, for example, may have hundreds of queens.

Worker ants may be the smallest, but they do the most work. All the workers are females. They care for the queen and her young. Worker ants build and repair the nest. They search for food and fight off enemies. Worker ants usually live one to five years.

Most male ants live only a few weeks or months. They do not work, and they die shortly after mating with young queens.

European wood
ant mound

What Does an Ant Nest Look Like?

Most ant species build underground nests. Worker ants dig tunnels and chambers, or rooms, in the soil. As the colony grows, workers add more tunnels and chambers to the nest.

Ant colonies can grow to be quite large. Some tropical ants build downward to make more room. Their nests may reach 20 feet (6 meters) below the ground. Others, such as European wood ants, build upward. They build huge mound nests that may be 5 feet (1.5 meters) tall. Then the ants connect the mounds with scent trails. The group of nests may cover an area as large as a tennis court. Millions of ants may live in these nests.

The chambers in an ant nest have many different uses. The queen has her own chamber for laying eggs. Some chambers are nurseries for the growing young. Food is stored in other chambers. Still other chambers are resting places for hard-working ants!

Diagram of Ant Nest

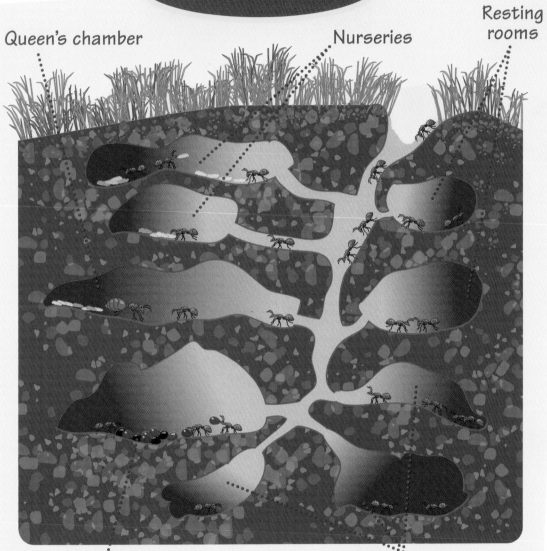

Queen's chamber

Nurseries

Resting rooms

Storage chamber

New rooms

15

How Does a Queen Ant Start a Colony?

Most species of ants start a new colony in the same way. A queen ant is born in one colony, but she usually leaves that colony to start a new one. As young queens grow, they develop wings. A few weeks after becoming adults, young queens fly out of the nest to mate with winged males. The queens then shed their wings and look for nesting places.

When a young queen finds a nesting spot, she builds a chamber and seals herself inside. Then she begins to lay eggs. The queen cares for the eggs, which develop into larvae *(LAHR vee)* and then pupae *(PYOO pee).* The queen feeds the young with her saliva. She does not eat during this time. Her body absorbs the unneeded wing muscles as food.

The eggs develop into small, female worker ants. Some of these workers leave the nest to find food for the colony. Others build onto the nest. The queen lays more eggs. Most develop into female workers. Others develop into males and young queens.

Ant queen with eggs and pupae

 17

What Do Worker Ants Do?

Worker ants work. And they work hard! All workers are females. But they very rarely become queens or reproduce. Instead, they care for the queen, the young ants, and the nest. Without its workers, an ant colony could not survive.

Worker ants may have one job or several jobs. They may keep the same job all their lives or change jobs from time to time. Some workers gather food for the colony. They store the food they harvest in special chambers in the nest. Other workers feed and care for the queen and her developing young. Still others build the chambers and tunnels. They use their saliva to make the dirt walls hard.

Some worker ants are soldiers. They defend the colony. In many species, soldier ants are larger than the other workers. The soldiers fight off enemy ants or insects. They may also use their large heads to block the entrances to the nest.

Worker ants
gathering seeds

Who Is Minding the Eggs?

Ants go through four different stages, or steps, of growth. These stages are egg, larva, pupa, and adult. Worker ants care for the young ants through each stage.

After a queen ant lays her eggs, worker ants take them to hatching chambers. There, the workers care for the eggs and often groom them by licking. The eggs hatch in a few days to become larvae. During the larvae stage, the young ants look like tiny white worms.

Worker ants move the larvae to new chambers and feed them for a few weeks until they become pupae. In some species, the larvae spin cocoons before they become pupae. In other species, the pupae are covered only by thin, see-through skin. Pupae do not eat or move. But they do change. In two to three weeks, adult ants come out of the cocoons or skin. They are now ready to go to work!

House ants with larvae

Why Do Ants Have Tiny Waists?

Ants have tiny waists so they can wriggle their end parts freely! An ant's waist has one or two movable parts. These parts allow the ant to twist and turn in different ways—an important feature for moving about an ant colony.

Ants have three main body parts: the head, the trunk, and the metasoma *(meht uh SOH muh)*. The ant's eyes, antennae, and mandibles *(MAN duh buhlz)* are located on its head.

Attached to the trunk are six legs with segments. Each leg has two claws at the foot. The claws hook into dirt, tree bark, or leaves, so ants can quickly walk, climb, and dig! Ants are strong, too. Many ants can lift 50 times their body weight!

The metasoma has two parts. They are the waist and the gaster. Organs for digesting, getting rid of waste, and reproducing are in the gaster. Some ant species have a sting at the end of the gaster to defend against other insects.

Diagram of Ant

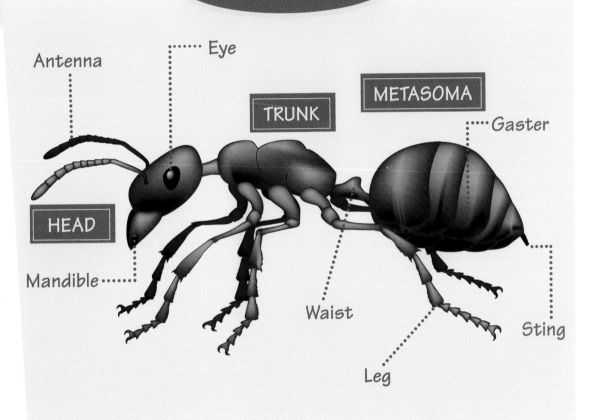

Antenna

Eye

METASOMA

TRUNK

Gaster

HEAD

Mandible

Waist

Leg

Sting

What Do Ants Eat?

Many ants eat fruit, flowers, and seeds. Others like honeydew, a juice made by some insects and plants. Some ants eat other insects. Still others eat everything in their path, including small animals.

Ants have special mouthparts for grabbing and eating food. First come the mandibles, which are jaws that move from side to side. Ants use their mandibles to hold food, carry their young, and fight enemies. Behind the mandibles are the maxillae *(mak SIHL ee)*, which are used for chewing. But ants do not swallow the food right away. First the food passes to a pouch behind the mouth. There, the liquid is squeezed out of the food. Ants swallow the liquid and spit out the leftover food pellet.

Ants have two kinds of stomachs—a stomach and a crop. Food an ant eats for itself goes to the stomach. Food it shares with others is stored in the crop. The ant spits up this food to feed other ants and larvae. Hungry ants may stroke each other or tap antennae to ask for food.

Wood ants dragging fly to nest

How Do Ants Recognize Each Other?

Ants in a colony have a special odor that helps them recognize one another. Outsiders or enemies have different odors. Soldier ants smell these invaders and kill them.

Ants do not have ears. They "hear" vibrations through their sense organs. An ant's antennae are its most important sense organ. Ants use their antennae to smell, touch, taste, and hear. It's easy to see why an ant's antennae are always moving. Antennae help ants find and taste food. They help ants recognize and touch one another. Antennae even help ants find their way.

Most ants have two compound eyes. A compound eye has many lenses. (A human eye has only one lens.) Because of their compound lenses, ants see things broken up, like an image in a kaleidoscope. Ants see movement better than shape.

Fighting ants

 27

Which Ants Herd the Aphids?

Dairying ants "herd" aphids *(AY fihdz)*—just as people herd cattle! The ants keep the aphids together and protect them from other insects. Why do the ants do this? It's because aphids produce something that the ants really like—honeydew. Aphids are small insects that suck plant juices and give off the excess as honeydew. Dairying ants eat the honeydew. They use their antennae to stroke the aphids, causing them to produce more of the sweet, sugary liquid.

Dairying ants take good care of their aphids. They will move their herd if the aphids need better plants to eat. They even store aphid eggs in their nests through the winter to start a new herd in the spring. A young queen may also take along an egg-laying aphid when she starts a new colony. This queen carries the aphid in her mandibles.

Ants herding aphids

29

Which Ants Farm the Fungus?

Leaf-cutter ants are farmers that grow their own food in underground gardens. The food they grow is a fungus, a kind of mold or mildew. The ants fertilize their fungus gardens with bits of leaves.

Leaf-cutters build huge colonies. Their nests can have a thousand chambers and tunnel down 20 feet (6 meters). Inside, up to a million ants may be at work!

Big and little ants are needed to farm the fungus. Large worker ants set out at night to gather leaves. They use their long, hooked mandibles to cut the leaves. Then they march back to the nest, holding the leaves high. For this reason, leaf-cutters are often called umbrella or parasol ants.

Inside the nest, smaller workers chew the leaves into a pulp, or paste. They put this paste on the fungus. Later, tiny ants harvest the fungus to feed the colony.

Leaf-cutter ants

Which Ants Are on the Move?

Army ants—thousands to millions of them—are almost always on the move! They do not build permanent nests. They just march along, carrying their young and looking for food. They kill and eat anything in their path. This usually includes spiders and other insects. But in some cases, army ants prey on larger animals that cannot get away quickly.

Each night, army ants do stop to rest. They gather together to form a cluster on a tree branch or in a log. The queen and the developing ants rest deep within the cluster, where they will be safe.

When the queen is laying eggs, the army ants cluster in the same spot each night. They remain at this temporary campsite until all the eggs have developed into active larvae. When the larvae begin to grow, the cluster moves to a new spot each evening.

Cluster of army ants

What Other Ways of Life Do Ants Have?

Ants have many different ways of life. Harvester ants gather seeds and store them in special chambers. When harvesters need food, they chew the seeds to make a pulp called ant bread. They squeeze the liquid out of this bread and swallow it for food.

Honey ants store their food, honeydew, in special workers. The workers store so much honeydew in their gasters that they cannot walk. They hang from the nest ceiling and spit up honeydew when other ants tap them.

Slave-maker ants steal pupae from other ants and raise them as their own. When the pupae develop, they work for the colony, digging tunnels and feeding the slave-makers.

Weaver ants build nests from leaves. To do this, some workers hold the sides of a leaf together. Others take silk-spinning larvae and pass them over the edges of the leaf to "weave" the edges together.

Weaver ants

What Is Buzzing in the Hive?

If you guessed bees, you were partly right. All bees make a buzzing sound, but only honey bees build hives. And honey bees stick together! Up to 80,000 of these hairy brown, black, and gold striped bees may live in a hive. In the wild, honey bees build hives in caves or hollow trees. Honey bees that people raise for their honey live in special hives that look like big boxes.

A honey bee hive is made up of layers of honeycombs. Each layer has many cells. Each cell is a hexagon. It has six equal sides. Eggs are placed in some of the cells. Pollen and honey are stored in other cells. The cells themselves are made of wax.

Honey bees eat lots of honey. Their bodies help turn the honey into wax. This wax oozes out in small flakes from their abdomens. Honey bees chew and knead the flakes. Then they press the "beeswax" to build new honeycomb cells.

Honey bees on honeycomb

How Do Honey Bees Live?

Like ants, honey bees live in a caste community. The queen bee has one job, to lay eggs. Drones are stingless males that live just long enough to mate with queens. The female workers do all the work!

In a hive, the queen bee lays eggs in brood cells. Workers feed royal jelly to newly hatched larvae. This creamy jelly is made by special glands in a worker bee's mouth. After two days, the workers begin to feed the larvae honey and pollen. (Larvae that are fed only royal jelly become queen bees.) Then the workers seal the larvae into the brood cells. There, the larvae turn into pupae and then into adult honey bees.

The first job of new workers is to clean the hive. Later, workers care for the young, gather food, and guard the hive. One defense a female worker has against enemies is a sting. A honey bee sting can be very painful to animals and people. But a honey bee sting is deadly for a honey bee. Honey bees die after using their stings.

Wild honey beehive

What Is So Sweet About Honey Bees?

Honey bees make enough honey for people to use. And that's sweet!

Honey bees visit as many as 1,000 flowers a day. They use their long tongues to sip nectar from the flowers. They store this nectar in their honey stomachs. The honey stomach is a special organ that breaks down the sugar in the nectar. When the bees return to the hive, they spit up the nectar. They give some of the nectar to other bees. The rest, they put into empty cells. That is where the nectar turns into sweet honey.

When a honey bee buzzes from flower to flower, it collects more than just nectar. Pollen sticks to its hairy body and hind legs. The bee brushes this pollen into "baskets," or sacs, on its hind legs. Later, when the bee returns to the hive, it kicks off the pollen into cells in the hive. Honey bees use this pollen as food.

Honey bee

Why Do Honey Bees Dance?

Honey bees dance to tell other bees where the food is. Some honey bee workers are scouts. They fly around looking for flowers full of nectar or pollen. When they find these flowers, they hurry to the hive with the news.

At the hive, honey bee scouts dance in a figure-eight pattern. As they dance, they make a line between the two loops of the figure eight. If the line points straight up the hive, then the flowers are located in the direction of the sun. A line pointing to the right means that the flowers are to the right of the sun. The line points left if the flowers are on the left of the sun. The faster the bees waggle their tails while they dance, the closer the flowers are.

Worker bees in the hive want to know all about the nectar that was found. They often tap the scout bees to signal for a sample. The scout bee then spits up some of the nectar for the worker bees to taste. If the worker bees like the sample, they all fly off to the flowers.

Honey bee
waggle dance

What Is Yellow and Black and Buzzes?

It may look like a honey bee, but it isn't. It's a bumble bee. Bumble bees are the larger, noisier cousins of honey bees. Bumble bees live in smaller colonies than honey bees. And they usually build nests, not hives.

Bumble bees do not have long-lasting colonies. In fact, only young queen bumble bees survive the winter. When spring comes, a young queen bumble bee crawls out of her hibernation place and looks for a place to build a nest. She might choose an old mouse hole or a clump of grass. Then she builds a little wax honey pot full of honey and nectar. The queen uses this food while she starts her colony.

Next, the queen builds a wax cell and lays a few eggs in it. These eggs develop into worker bumble bees. Some workers fly off to gather food. Others start expanding the nest. The queen bee stays in the nest and keeps on laying eggs.

Bumble bee

What Do Bumble Bees Drink?

Bumble bees, like other bees and wasps, sip nectar. Nectar is that sweet liquid made by flowering plants. Bumble bees have long tongues that can reach deep into flowers of red clover, vetch, and honeysuckle.

While the bumble bees drink the nectar, they also gather pollen from the plants. As they fly from flower to flower, some of the pollen falls off the bees and back onto the plants. This pollinates, or fertilizes, the plants so that they can produce seeds and spread. This, in turn, makes farmers very happy. They use these plants to feed their livestock.

Bumble bee sipping nectar

Where Do Paper Wasps Live?

Paper wasps live in paper nests, of course! These slender, reddish-brown social insects are incredible architects. Their nests usually hang from a tree or a porch. The openings face downward to keep out the rain.

Paper wasps make their own building materials. Female wasps chew up plant parts or old wood. They mix this with saliva to make thin paperlike layers. The wasps then paste the paper together to make the open cells of the nest. The wasps lay their eggs in these cells.

Paper wasps capture caterpillars and other insects. They chew up the meat of these animals to make food paste that they feed to their young larvae. Adult wasps feed themselves flower nectar.

Paper wasp and nest

What Is on a Yellow Jacket's Menu?

A yellow jacket—a type of small wasp with black and yellow markings—usually feeds on nectar and fruits. And, like paper wasps, yellow jackets chew meats and feed the paste to their larvae. Yellow jackets also engage in mutual feeding. When they feed the larvae, the larvae produce a drop of saliva for the adult wasps to eat.

Some species of yellow jackets feed on dead animal matter. These wasps are often uninvited guests at picnics. They have come to feed on the sweet fruit and soda and the sandwich meat.

Yellow jackets belong to the same family of wasps as hornets. Both kinds of wasps build paper nests. Most yellow jackets nest underground or in places like hollow walls. Most hornet nests hang in bushes or trees. Both kinds of wasps are very protective of their nests. If anyone disturbs the nest, worker wasps will sting over and over again!

Yellow jackets and nest

What Are Termites?

Termites are social insects that look a lot like ants. In fact, some people used to call them white ants. But termites are more closely related to cockroaches than to ants. So, how can you tell termites from ants? Look at their waists. Termites have thick waists, not tiny "ant waists."

Termite colonies are made up of both male and female termites. The highest class is the royals, or the king and queen. Only the royals reproduce. They live in the royal chamber where the queen's body swells to hold thousands of eggs.

Blind, wingless workers feed the royals. They tend the eggs and feed the growing larvae. They also build the chambers and tunnels and bring in food.

Soldier termites defend the nest. They have big, hard heads and strong legs. When enemy ants approach, the soldiers rush out, jaws snapping. Although soldiers defend the nest, they cannot take care of themselves. Worker termites feed them.

Termites on a fence

53

How High Is a Termite Tower?

Most species of termites tunnel down, building nests underground or in trees or wood buildings. But some species build up! These master builders live in Africa, Australia, Asia, and South America. Some build towers up to 25 feet (7.5 meters) high.

How do termites build towers? When termites dig, they bring the soil to the surface. They mix their saliva with the soil so that it hardens. The more soil the termites dig, the higher the tower grows.

Termite towers have a special purpose: to warm and cool the nest. Australian compass termites build towers with flat sides that face north and south. The flat sides catch the sun's rays in the morning and evening to warm the nest. The pointed top deflects the hot noonday sun.

The fungus-growing termites of Africa have towers that are mostly hollow. Hollow towers act like chimneys, letting the hot air rise. Small tunnels down the sides let fresh air in, keeping the queen cool.

Termite tower

What Does Swarming Mean?

Social insects do many things together, including swarming! When insects swarm, they move or fly off together in large groups. Insects have several reasons for swarming. They swarm when it's time to start a new colony. They swarm if their nest is disturbed. They also swarm during mating flights.

When a bee colony becomes overcrowded, hundreds of worker bees fly off with their old queen. They gather on tree branches, posts, and even street lamps. A few scouts fly off, looking for a new home. When they find it, they return and do a bee dance to share the news.

When the old queen leaves, young queens are left behind to take over egg-laying duties in the old colony. Sometimes, a few of these young queens may also leave with a small group of workers to start their own colonies. Wasps do this, too.

Termites and most ants swarm when young queens and males set off on their mating flights.

Bees swarming

How Do Social Insects Help Us?

Social insects help people in many ways. Some eat dead plants and animals. They help the dead matter decay, adding minerals to the soil. Ants and termites also loosen the soil, which helps water reach plant roots.

Some wasps and ants eat insects that are harmful to crops. By eating these insects, wasps and ants help keep the numbers of the pests in check.

Bees help farmers by pollinating plants. They also provide honey and beeswax. Scientists are trying to learn how to use bee sting venom as medicine.

There are times, however, when social insects are too social. Termites may nest in wood, causing it to rot. Some wasps nest around homes, becoming stinging pests. Some ants ruin crops. In the United States, fire ant mounds make it difficult to cut hay. Fire ants also have a painful sting. In Brazil, leaf-cutter ants can strip the leaves from an orange grove in one night!

Wasp with caterpillar

Are Social Insects in Danger?

For the most part, social insects are not in danger. Their numbers are in the millions. And they reproduce at such a fast rate that they are not in danger of extinction. But these insects do face some dangers.

People often use strong chemicals to control insect pests. These pesticides can be dangerous to other insects, animals, plants, and the soil. They destroy both harmful and helpful insects.

Changes in the environment affect insects, just as they do all living things. But there are millions and millions of social insects. They will be creeping, crawling, and flying for a long time to come!

Red ant

Social Insect Fun Facts

→ Some ants can survive up to 14 days underwater! This is a useful trait for ants that live in flood plains.

→ European colonists first brought honey bees to the Americas in the 17th century.

→ Social insects appear in moral tales because of their industrious way of life. Guess which insect has food for the winter in Aesop's fable "The Grasshopper and the Ant."

→ Fossils of ants show that they have lived on the earth for more than 100 million years.

→ A termite queen is like an egg factory. She lays between 5,000 and 30,000 eggs a day!

→ Utah is nicknamed the *Beehive State.*

→ Some soldier ants really know how to use their heads. They protect their nests against attack by plugging up the entrances with their heads!

→ The honey bee is the state insect of 10 states: Arkansas, Maine, Mississippi, Missouri, New Jersey, Oklahoma, South Dakota, Utah, Vermont, and Wisconsin.

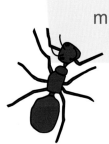

Glossary

adult Final stage of insect development.

antennae Jointed insect feelers.

aphid Small insect that sucks sap from plants.

cocoon Silky case spun by some ants to live in as they grow.

colony Nest home of social insects.

drone Male honey bees.

fungus A group of nongreen plants, such as mushrooms, that have no flowers or leaves.

honeycomb A wax structure made by bees to store their honey in.

honeydew Sweet, sticky liquid given off by aphids and some other insects.

larva Wormlike stage of insect development, between egg and pupa. The plural is *larvae.*

mandibles Pair of jaws that move from side to side. Ants use them for grasping, carrying, fighting, and digging.

maxillae Mouth parts used for chewing by ants.

nectar Sweet liquid produced by some plants.

pollen Tiny yellow grains produced by plants.

pollinate To fertilize plants so that they reproduce.

pupa Inactive stage of insect development, between larva and adult. The plural is pupae.

queen Female, egg-laying insect in a colony of social insects.

saliva Liquid produced in the mouth that helps digestion.

social insects Insects that breed, live, and work together.

swarm To leave the hive or nests in a large group.

vetch A climbing herb grown as feed for cattle and sheep.

waggle To move quickly from side to side; to move one's tail.

Index

(**Boldface** indicates a photo, map, or illustration.)

For more information about social insects, try these resources:

The Honey Makers, by Gail Gibbons, Harper Trophy, 2000

Inside an Ant Colony, by Allan Fowler, Children's Press, 1998

The Life and Times of the Honeybee, by Charles Micucci, Houghton Mifflin Co., 1997

http://myrmecology.org/

http://www.insects.org/entophiles/hymenoptera/index.html

http://www.pbs.org/wgbh/nova/bees/

Social Insect Classification

Scientists classify animals by placing them into groups. The animal kingdom is a group that contains all the world's animals. Phylum, class, order, and family are smaller groups. Each phylum contains many classes. A class contains orders, an order contains families, and a family contains individual species. Each species also has its own scientific name. Here is how the animals in this book fit in to this system.

Insects and their relatives (Phylum Arthropoda)

Insects (Class Insecta)

Ants, bees, wasps, and their relatives (Order Hymenoptera)

Ants (Family Formicidae)

Bumble bees, honey bees, and their relatives (Family Apidae)

Honey bee.................................... *Apis mellifera*

Hornets, paper wasps, yellowjackets, and their relatives (Family Vespidae)

Termites (Order Isoptera)

In many species of animals, a common name corresponds to a single scientific name. For example, the honey bee has the scientific name Apis mellifera. However, there are so many species of social insects that some of them share the same common name. For example, there are many different species of ants called dairying, leaf-cutter, or weaver ants.